all the way to just about there

Sandra S. McRae

FUTURECYCLE PRESS
www.futurecycle.org

Cover artwork, "Abstract Jupiter Atmosphere" from the Perijove 10 Mission, NASA, with oil painting filter by Rick Lundh; author photo by Sarah Sajbel; cover and interior book design by Diane Kistner; Georgia text and Gill Sans titling

Library of Congress Control Number: 2019940361

Published by FutureCycle Press
Athens, Georgia, USA

ISBN 978-1-942371-75-5

for Joe, Sarah, and Lily...
remember to look up

Contents

appetites and insights

can I get a witness?

all the way to just about there

prologue

Mama Returns from the Morning Dash to the Bus Stop

Let the laundry sit in rumpled clumps on the sofa
wringing its wrinkled hands.

Let the coffee table sag reproachfully
laden with half-empty mugs and wadded napkins.

Leave the plates with their abandoned waffle crusts
adrift on the counter tiles

the half-eaten strawberries clinging to the ceramic
in a shriveled embrace.

Spoons, knives, milk-filmed glasses—they can sit.
Let the pots huddle neglected in the sink.

The salt crystals can mingle with the dried tomato leaves
in awkward silence on the table

while the fruit flies gossip over the cantaloupe.
I don't care.

The Saran Wrap and Ziplocs lie scattered
about the cutting board

the aftermath of a horrible accident, it seems
the crumb outline

of where the sandwich met its terrible demise.
Everything stares in a crescendo of guilt.

To all of it I say:

You can just wait—
        I have something to say.

stories and portraits

A Child's Pink Suitcase Full of Used Hypodermics

lies about 50 yards below the road
where it has slid

down the steep slope and into a tree.
It rests peacefully on its back

peeking out of the snow
in the bright sunshine

shiny gold zipper
twinkling across the expanse of pink.

Cheerful pose
compared to what's inside:

plastic gallon bags crammed full of
needles used by God knows who.

Did I say needles?
What I meant was

nestled inside that suitcase
in a styrofoam block

are two bottles of 1982 Château La Tour
and a handful of loose diamonds

tossed in as an afterthought.
Good thing it's spring

season of melt and more wine-friendly temps
and anyway it doesn't matter

because what's inside that case
is a small but sturdy

scale model of our dream home
with absolutely no sides facing north

just east, south, west.
You know, the big white house with the lilac trim

wide, welcoming steps
and long, curved porch with

porch swing on the left, rockers on the right
and windows! windows! windows!

Also inside there
is the treasure map to the shallow spot

where the chest of gold coins to pay for all this
lies buried

and that's good, because we're going to need
money—a lot of money—

because inside that pink suitcase
is an entire tropical seaport

where the tourists arrive daily by cruise ship
hundreds of them streaming out of its great white bulk

clattering up the planks of the docks in their sunhats
and they're hungry! They want Mexican food

of exceptional freshness, generous drinks
perfectly balanced between sweet and tart

delivered by smiling waiters
in colorful print shirts

who hustle beneath the picado banners
and the slow-spinning fans

as the laughter spills out
the wide-open shutters

down the tile steps
into the daylight, the sunset

the star-speckled night
where the waves lap at the shore

chuckling softly over what a truly
marvelous day this has been.

Stories

In our stories we're always the heroes
    slaying our attackers with the perfect retort

flipping off the evil-doers
    bombing the insurgents to rubble.

We practically dash into burning buildings
    to rescue the baby in the nick of time.

We're always the life of the party
    the smooth operator
        the high adventurer
            maybe a naughty bandito.

In our youth we were the sly graffiti artist
    rowdy liquor lord
        slippery sex god.

And way back when?
    Radiant fashion queen
        playground Olympian.

And then there was the time we got lost in Paris
Budapest   Mexico City   took the wrong bus
and found not only Shangri-La but El Dorado too
and lived to tell about it—here, check out this artifact.

We outfoxed the hustler in the village bazaar—
    oh, we had that car salesman back-pedaling
and that claims adjuster? Caught him in a lie and won the lawsuit
    yippee-ki-yi-yay.

So what.
I want the stories of the time you knew but didn't tell
because you relished the power of a secret.
How you stuck to your story
and someone who really couldn't afford to
took the fall.

The time you beat up the skinny kid
　　　left him crying in the dirt, when you
told that bitch where she could stick it
because her fierceness scared you.

Let's hear about the time you lifted some bills from the petty cash
left the scene of the accident because you were fucked up
　　　and besides
　　　no one saw.

Or that friend you flailed in a drunken rage—
　　　you were such an ass
　　　but didn't care, didn't stop.
How years later you read in the paper
　　　of her death by a swift-moving cancer.

Tell me, up close, about the bedroom betrayal
how surprisingly easy it was
to live with.

The child you screamed at
and maybe even shook.
How about that daddy complex?

Spill: your shabbiest moments
　　　　　your twisted fetish
　　　　　　　　your covetous hollow

all the tears you ever caused.

Those stories. I want those.

Bombs Over Baghdad

for Mustafa and his family

I put on my coat
as the news anchor announced
the assault had started.
I couldn't bear to listen.

Outside.
Seven feet of snow and still falling.
Cozy white settling over Colorado
a blanket of fire dropped over Baghdad.
I was ready to put in another hour
shoveling the driveway.
The snow was so deep
blue light filled the holes my feet left
as I climbed the white pile
that was once a set of stairs.

I couldn't move the snow.
There was nowhere to put it.
There was nowhere to house reason
nowhere to tuck a prayer.
I stopped.
The planes had all been grounded
the highway closed.
I could hear the snowflakes landing on my coat.
I stood there, listening.
I watched the flakes pile up on me
knowing that others burned in my name.

Blood on the Motel Sidewalk

In the flat January morning light
it looks like scattered coins
each fat drop a perfect circle.
You might feel lucky walking up from afar
eager to tally your find.
But as you bent to pick up your dark fortune
you'd stop.
Not coins but blood, bold punctuation of disaster.
A story.
And looking closer, each one oddly flecked
with white grains of salt.
And then you might notice the scatter
of asparagus and potatoes
—this is an odd tale—
wondering what transpired
in the fluorescent night where
you now recall from your cottony
motel slumber
voices outside the window
rushed but calm
calling for help, then for towels
then a car pulling up
and headlights dragging across the ceiling
as you rolled back over onto your side
grateful for the sudden return
of quiet.

In Deutschland

In Germany
    the phone booths
    were bright yellow
the color of an emergency
    which it always was
the color of caution
    which I never exercised
and now I know
    the color
    of the stain
    that money leaves
    after it's gone.

The phone booths
    at the train stations
    were the worst—
always cold, always filthy.
Sometimes there was a booth on the platform.
If you were using one of these
    you really were desperate—
    desperately hoping someone would change their mind
    desperately seeking someone who should have stepped off
    the 15:05.
Or maybe you just forgot to feed the cat
    and wanted the neighbor to check in
but chances are you weren't so lucky
    if you were standing there
    on the frosty side of the glass
where some other poor soul
had left a pile of used tissues on the floor.

In the Schildergasse in Köln
    halfway down
    on the left
    as you walk toward the Neumarkt

there were three half-booths
    just the right size for a quick call
    to ask what was on that shopping list
    you left at home
or to tell them when to expect you for dinner
or just a quick check-in ending with a friendly
Tschüß as quick and sweet as a peck on the lips.
There was a church there, too, just in case.

But the phone booth in the middle of the plaza
    at the center of Hürth
    where I lived without you
    and then in spite of you
was the loneliest of all
    where the Groschen echoed mightily
    as they slid down down down
    to the bottom of the Atlantic
and the speaker drew sharp breaths
    adrift in a sea of stones
    announced with a sail of bright yellow
    a sorry target
    for pirates
    seagulls
    and other scavengers.

Ode to Disease

Let us sing a song of praise to Disease
industrious worker in the kingdoms
    of faith and science.
Sing of how it fills the halls of research
with full- and part-time employ
    the pastor's schedule
    with appointments long and productive.
How it brings the faithful to their knees
the donors to the galas.
Ever whirring in the background
or breeding silently as cells gone haywire
with a mad, internal Spring
    Disease burns like a star
    in the universe of the body.

Let us hail the man with a collection of lungs
he studies to unlock the mysteries of demise.
The moist sacks hang in glass jars
where twin tubes run into each pair.
He flips a switch so they can
    inflate...deflate
    inflate...deflate.
Some struggle
some all but refuse
but one pink pair
gladly comply.
    These are his favorites
eager partners in a vital enterprise
    flawless fraternal twins
    born under a lucky sign.
Ever willing to pitch in
they divide their work as in life
    where they rose to every occasion
    with synchronized grace.

The man knows he owes a debt
to their crippled, reluctant brethren—
     the blackened, the spotted, the shriveled.
But he remembers how these two
once gently cupped their heart
folded around it like angel wings.

     Working late
the man thinks of all the other organs
Disease washes up on the shores of inquiry—
     hearts, livers, kidneys brought forth
     on a dark and generous tide.
Harvested from night, in the light of day they sprout
campaigns, foundations, dissertations—
fruitful labor for the devout.

     The night breathes on.
He marvels at how Disease crowds first into cells
then thoughts, then dreams
of the simple and learned alike
     how it teaches the weak to hope
     the strong to bend to a fickle and demanding will
     the way Disease can make even the tight-lipped
     open their mouths to God.

This Is What She Did

When the rain came
she wrapped herself in wool and black

and walked with an umbrella
to the cemetery two bus stops away.

Under the bare lindens
she opened the lantern bejeweled with raindrops

replaced the stub of red candle
with a new one

her bare white hands
nimble for the task.

Nestled in the glass and metal box
the candle awaited her offering.

She reached into her pocket for the matches.
With a scratch and a sputter   she lit the candle

its flame flaring in defiance of the grey sky
the drizzling opposition to warmth

and closed the small door of the lantern.
She rose slowly

brushed the dampness off her knees
folded her hands before her

bowed her head
prayed.

She did not pray with words or recitations
but buried her mouth in her scarf

imagined the warmth of her own breath
the heat from his body on a cold winter night.

After a few moments   she lifted her head
turned   walked home

the tiny white flame
behind her   burning on.

Winter Walk (Ambuscade)

Sometimes when walking alone
beneath the huddled grey
of a late-December afternoon
air so cold I can see my breath
     the post-holiday letdown
     holding its edge of despair
     to my throat
I remember him.

Tenth grade.
We met on the bridge over the creek
that separated our neighborhoods.
He needed to talk
but it was awkward there
above the icy trickle
the dead leaves frozen in the mud.
We had nothing in common
except my best friend
who had dumped him just before Christmas.
I don't think I'd ever
looked into his face
because it was usually in her face
at our locker where I always had to wait
as he kissed her like he eventually
kissed everyone: diligent
intent on perfecting his technique.

We walked along
until he stopped
locked eyes on me
and asked if I would be his girlfriend.

Now here is where the poem could end.
Me indignant, righteous
and even hostile.

Me too self-assured
to play the pawn
in a silly drama.

Me being anyone
other than
the girl
who was too polite
and lonely
to say no.

La Femme Nikita and Her Sisters

      If you are to believe
the world as depicted in grey-toned thrillers
set in overcast cities on the brink of December
      then you would have to *not* be surprised
that the scrawny but strangely beautiful
doe-eyed, leather-clad street waif
      who haunts the banks
      of the Seine/Thames/Nieva/Hudson/Moskva
in search of bad ex-boyfriends, street drugs, or maybe even
a waitressing gig in some dive where the tips are mostly
half-smoked Gitanes/Stuyvesants or subway tokens
      —so she can't scrape together
      une seule centime/a single dime/a bloody kopek
      for bread or even coffee—
is somehow wearing
(underneath that oversized black sweater
that dwarfs her slender shoulders and sleek feline
      composure)
several hundred dollars' worth
of the most stunning designer lingerie
pinched from some Paris/London/Village/Tretyakovsky boutique
      and that most conveniently enhances
      her surprisingly curvaceous features
just in case a Harrison Ford/Matt Damon/Robert Redford type
might accidentally meet and/or need to kidnap her outside, say
      a boulangerie/teahouse/coffee shop/pub
where—it just so happens—she's been waiting
to pickpocket some poor old sap just draining his cup
      (an unremarkable yet vaguely dapper gent)
who turns out to be a Russian spy/British mole/former CIA
      operative turned traitor/arms dealer/art thief
on his way to or from a major heist
of global consequence
      and

at the precise moment she brushes against said geezer
  and unwittingly swipes the secret code/safe
  deposit key/computer chip
that holds the entire fate of the free world in the balance
  you know—just *know*—that the inevitable stress
  of kidnapping/being kidnapped
and being subsequently chased down dank alleys at top speed
  or skittering across the city rooftops
  swinging from rainspout to fire escape
under the deadly gaze of a sharpshooter's high-power rifle scope
  will eventually wear down
our hapless heroine and her equally victimized captor/hero
until the only solace they can find
  in the mean streets of Paris/London/New York/Moscow
is a damp and furtive yet exquisitely passionate
roll in some fleabag hotel
  which ultimately reminds us that
even if
  the KGB/CIA/diamond cartel/drug lords of South America
can't wait to splatter your guts
across some dingy tenement stairwell and shut you up forever
  it is good to be loved
if only just once
by a perfect stranger
who is sort of your enemy
but really your only ally/hope for survival and that
  Mom was right
when she said
always wear clean underwear
you never know what might happen today.

For Sarah, Driving to the PSAT

Sometimes this love is a fist
squeezing my heart

catching me off guard in an ordinary gesture
      as you turn your shoulders to reach for a pencil
            or bow your head over books as in prayer

and now as—hands at 10 and 2—you
steer cautiously into your future.
How could you be so wholly beautiful
sweet child of mine?

You tell me how it is possible
that I can't remember the names of streets where I have lived
      entire years of my sinuous life
            —even where I put my glasses just minutes ago—

and yet your voice when you were three
rings clear as birdsong
through the cavern of my skull.

How love has wrought an indelible record
of those finger-paint handprints, those swing-set squeals
every puffed cheek that ever hovered over birthday candles.

How it still makes each sunrise marbled and beautiful and vibrant
      as the wonder I felt
            the first time I saw your face.

I Tell Her Every Day She's Beautiful

but she can't hear me
as she watches pouty pop stars
with sassy accessories
and the cosmetics that promise to trade her "puffy eyes"
and "poofy hair" for confidence.

Let's go for a walk.
The continental divide stretches like a cat before us.
Snowfall skirts the trees, dazzles their branches.
The dogs run ahead, then back
goofy bliss blazing their muzzles
and finally she laughs.

I'm reminded that 13 is a disease
for which the only cure is 14

and then there's *that* lake of woes to cross
until, like a distant shore, 15 offers some respite

before 16 appears like a steamship you can't wait to board
and then you're off, free at last.

See? I say. *I told you beauty bubbles up from the inside out.*

She rolls her eyes
says something about my "Mom goggles."
But her shoulders lower ever so slightly
and she knows I'll repeat it
until finally she gets it.
I won't stop until she gets it.

Where I Come From

—after F. Isabel Campoy

I come from a fledgling suburb
in a state that lost its mind with beauty
and had to cope by building tract homes and strip malls.
Where I come from, everyone calls out to friends
from patios studded with braziers
across yards littered with bicycles
sandboxes and panting mutts.
Cookouts there are a seasonal language
but by July everyone is fluent
in potato salad.

I come from slopes of purple-flecked bindweed
and drainage ditches where we scour for crawdads
hiding in the shade of scraggly Russian olives.
We sneeze until October.

I come from a living room framed
by a jumble of scratchy couches.
The green one hides a sofa bed
because it is good to have space
for visitors.
Relatives arrive
with train cases and presents
speaking Italian loudly.
They do yoga right there in the front room
until we drag them into the kitchen
for honey buns and card games.
They dole out dollar bills from leather coin purses
that look like the money pouches
carried in fairy tales.

Where I come from
kids shoot out of back doors like rockets
and race to the park.

The hot metal bars of the jungle gym sear our palms
until we give up and run for Icees at the 7-Eleven.
Domes of cherry sweetness tower over
the curled edges of the waxed paper cups
and drops of condensation
slide down the sides
cooling our blisters.
We only stop talking when a frosty gulp
gives us a friendly punch in the throat
as if to say: *You're all right, kid.*

Where I come from, the evenings are perfumed with anise
as steam rises from the pizzelle iron
or *ciamello* bakes in the oven.
On the stove salted water simmers a warm welcome
to homemade ravioli
that slide eagerly into its open arms.
Their love is consummated in *sugo alla Napoletano.*

Where I come from
bath time is a necessary evil
but we strip and slip into the hot water
anyway. It stings the raw spot
between our toes
where the rubber thongs of flip-flops
are doing their best to toughen us
for the long haul.
There are band-aids and sunburns
in our future, but first
clean jammies
cool sheets
and sweet dreams
of where we're going.

carpe tempestas

January: Ludicrous Blue

If you were to paint a landscape
with a sky this color

curators would point to it
as evidence of the artist's insanity.

Beset with an irrational optimism
they might say...or *Clearly beyond*

the bounds of delusion itself.
Even *Tragically hopeful*

in a time of global unrest.
Yes, it's that boggling a hue.

A blue that only occurs near polar ice caps
or when the temperature up here

dips so far below zero
even the sun is amused.

The snow underfoot
squeaks in appreciation.

Pines wave their arms
and toss silver glitter.

The only clouds
are the billowing trails from tailpipes

as we crunch our way down the mountain
bristled awake

to the glorious potential
of our long-term prospects.

February

When we walked out of the vet's office
the snow was blowing sideways—
blasts of mock confetti.
The wind had been howling for days
roughing up our dog, parting her fur
in brutal slices as she crouched feebly in the snow
while I stood sentinel, unable to block the gusts.
It had paused just long enough for us to gently
usher her into that final appointment
a family bound in anguish and tenderness.
Now this heaving insult.

"Last one out shuts off the lights," we used to say at camp
and as we left the vet's
the sky was bleak, a stunned white wild with grief.
Everything mourning but this profane wind
harassing us all the way to the car
where we slammed ourselves in
gusts rocking our metal shelter
while snowflakes swirled madly before settling on our coats.
Sobbing, little Lily bleated her sorrow
as we pulled away: *Em-i-ly! Em-i-ly!*
The wind wailed on, slicking all the roads
throwing up snow blinds at every curve.
Steering through a screen of tears
we slid, skimming the ditch
on the last bend before home.

Now it just won't stop being February.
It grinds on like a glacier
and I want to strangle ugly February
stubby little month with the Napoleon complex
killing everyone I ever loved

and now sweet Emily.
February, I can't wait to beat you with the rock of March
grind your black soul into moss and daffodils
something soft and relenting.

March at 8,500 Feet

I live where all the east-facing street signs
are buckled at the bolts
      where the wind has been trying for months
           to tear them from their posts.

Every so often
the wind prevails.

Last spring it was the Highway 74 sign
      at Squaw Pass. It spun and waved
          on its tenuous strip of metal
             a ninja star bent on mayhem.

That one's gonna kill someone
I told dispatch. This winter

      an I-70 marker at exit 248 disappeared.

A county ordinance
at the bus stop
      CLEAR CREEK COUNTY SHERIFF
      FORBIDS THE DISCHARGE OF FIREARMS
landed in the tall dry grass of November.

Today street names here and there
hang limp as fortune cookie paper.

But now it is March
      first day of spring
         and I am amazed
            we've weathered another one.

I cannot say how many feet of snow we shoveled.
It doesn't matter.
Other towns had it worse.
There's a road in Park County
still buried under a three-foot drift.
And more wind in the forecast.

But I can see blue
and the snow going brown
in a blush of dirt and shame
as if it couldn't help itself.

It's okay, I whisper. *It's in your nature.*

In April

In April we leave the window blinds open at night
regardless of the temperature.

In December we seal every pane by 5:00
and hunker down in our leather bunker for the night

but by April we are sick of the dark and cold.
We crave light and lingering sunsets.

We'll take any last photon that might care to bounce our way
leave a light on for it.

Instead we get snow hurled at the glass
big wet pellets

or flaky sheets whipping in our faces
but we refuse to block out

its overripe welcome
determined to stare it down

until it breaks out in a purple blush
of crocus.

May in Evergreen

There once were four seasons
all in their places.
Now bold storms blow in
and each gale erases
the last hour's glimmer
of sunshine and hope
and wet, heavy snow
coats every slope.

June Wedding

This is the day we thought would never come.

Warm yellow light rolls down the mountain
as the sun climbs the rain-washed sky.

Pines stand proud and poised
holding the bright green tips of their branches

out to the breeze
like bridesmaids who've just had their nails done.

The granite peak hulks in reverent silence
having cleared its throat of words centuries ago.

Lining the road are stands of yellow pea flowers
that have blossomed overnight as if on cue.

A chorus of ravens starts up
accompanied by the chitter of squirrels.

I'm ready. We're all ready.
I take that first step, a perfect foot strike

and run the very edge of the road
the shoulder beside the drop-off

a gandy dancer working the line
between the created and the made

racing toward my first true love
this beautiful fresh Creation.

July Storm

All day the house heaved with heat
panting like the dog who kept
pacing the living room, shoulders heavy
with the dropping pressure
the nervous doom of thunder.

Was it just me
or did dinner taste flat too?

What a relief
when night fell
and the air crackled
with the authority of Zeus
whose booming voice
shut out the lights.

Now we have front-row
mountaintop seats.
In our third-floor bathroom
we sit along the edge of the empty tub
     kids in the middle
and watch the spectacle through the window before us.
Across the valley
fireworks arc above distant peaks.
Four chubby feet swing above the fiberglass.
Four long ones slap the white in appreciative applause.
The window opens its wide eye and
—thirsty for the next big thrill—
we lap at the snarls of light.

They must be crazy down in the city
dodging through the rain in a dash to the car
then squinting at streetlights
through a screen of water.

All those people with something to do.
Lucky us, we say as we retire to the big bed
to snuggle like puppies
and watch the rest of the show
safe and dry
together.

August: Back to School

This is the month of surrender
that graceful arc often mistaken for giving up.
It's the time of craving completeness
but something keeps tugging at the other end of the day
like a dog pulling the covers off
when all you want
is to go on sleeping
cocooned in warmth.

And now the sun begins
to slowly murder the aspen
tilting away to another hemisphere
breaking the hearts of all who behold
green blushing to gold.

And now time starts pilfering coins
right out of your pocket
but you think it's only the breeze
as you reach for the peaches
the ripe, juicy peaches
dreaming of pies.

September Sprint

Slow down, September.
You're always dashing in and out of here
before I can get enough of you.

Look at you, so fresh and alive
rushing toward adolescence and your cool new friends.
Even the trout leap out of their chilly lakes
to get a better glimpse of you.
Slow down.
Make them do that again.

But why would you? Isn't youth wasted
on the gorgeous? You can't wait
to shimmy out of these glorious duds
and disappear into the fog
skinny-dipping in the frosty breeze.
And then you'll be off to the next dance
gone in a swirl
of snowflakes
leaving me
wanting more.

October Aspens

Early evening and the air is giddy with color
as waning light sets the hillside ablaze:
orange flames   lick thickets of gold.

A puff of wind
and the quaking rustles

sets a million golden leaves flapping
        in dappled applause.

I stoop to scoop these coins
        the breeze has generously scattered.

Some, veins still plump with life,
        are studded with dew diamonds.
Tomorrow, wherever their delicate velvet
        has rested on the graveled road
black snowflakes will blossom
then spread like flowers to decay.

But today the world is aflame with hope

        every cell
        pulsing with sap

        singing this splendor
                this perfect
                vibrant
                moment.

November: Hibernation Song

Late fall and I want to eat—
pillage forests and late-night kitchens
in a desperate quest for calories—
>   then slip
>   into
>   a deep, narcotic slumber
> induced by hormones and sanctioned by God.

I wanna be Mama Bear—roly-poly, tummy out to there!
Mama Bear, snacking on pears ripe and juicy
smacking up berries sweet and fruity, packing on the
hazelnuts, apples—marshmallows found in a camper's stash.

Forget the fat ripe melons of summer.
Their cast-off rinds are just sarcastic smiles
from the compost heap now.
>   I want the good stuff:
fluffy buttermilk biscuits smothered in sausage gravy

steaming cheese grits whipped up into a cheddar frenzy
garlic mashed potatoes glistening with pools of melted butter

great lumps of lobster meat drenched in Alfredo sauce
slithering down an orgy of spaghetti strands

towers of Belgian waffles crowned with mounds of whipped cream
massive slabs of coconut cream pie

a heap of hot fresh jelly donuts crusted with sugar crystals
great blobs of raspberry jam buried in their bellies.

And yes! the beignets, the Hollandaise
the exquisite rapture of pastry glaze!

Let me die like this
the soft kiss of meringue
still lingering on my lips.

December Epiphany

I had made a change
—who knows if it was intentional or not—

and suddenly it was December again
the sun noncommittal and aloof.

Who was I to argue?

I was thinking of getting fat
—just lying on the couch and eating cookies.

Let middle age have the final say
instead of this constant bickering.

I was contemplating a life of crime
how long I could get away with it.

I was fed up with the most recent
economic collapse

and how it affected everyone but the super-rich
who had caused this one too.

I wondered if stealing from them to give to the poor
would stand the 21st-century test of morality—whatever that was.

Then I got bored thinking about it
and the dog gave me a nudge in the armpit

and it seemed a better use of my time
to go for a walk and think about the good stuff

the miracles we never say thanks for
like sky and water and even this damn wind

that means warmer weather is moving in
which is the opposite of what you're supposed to get

in December
which was probably the point.

Deciduous Wisdom

Winter

Look up through its branches
and it fractures the big blue bowl of the sky.
On grey days it's the spider-web snag
in the tarp of atmosphere.

Spring

Hanging from that network
are lovely ornaments
to distract you
from your quotidian pain:
buds, nascent leaves, a crystal globe of sap
—the miracle of a bird's nest.

Summer

A tree will always open its arms to you,
welcome you into the sanctum of its shade
the wonder of its heights.

Fall

A tree takes seasons in stride
slows the swift rush of time
by sticking its hands into the current
feeling every detail
until strangeness becomes familiar.

Always

A tree is an excellent listener.
Its advice is whispered in code.
Hold still. You'll get it.

appetites and insights

The Secret Life of Groceries

All those beans in cans
sleeping in the dark

shoulder to shoulder
belly to tail.

All those corn kernels
packed into steel

waiting to spill forth
bright and crisp

as the day they were
incarcerated.

Bread-n-butter pickles
bobbing in sugary brine

yearning to escape
that tiny eddy of detention.

And milk
envious of every waterfall

corralled in its square silo
yearning to burst free

if only to perish on its own terms
rushing across the floor

thinning itself
to a pale white sheen.

It will die trying to make its way home to the cow.

Call Now and Receive This Classic 4-DVD Set!

PBS wants my money
but Julia Child

wants my personal happiness.
Today she would like to ensure it herself

by demonstrating, with casual but unmistakable skill
how to achieve that classic of French simplicity

the two-egg *omelette*.
No *fromage* even..."no need for it."

Simply eggs, butter, salt, pepper
and that most elusive of ingredients:
      le technique juste.

Of course, once this timeless delight is plated
and sprinkled with fresh garden-grown thyme

I'll be implored to open my wallet
for public television and all this priceless programming.

And, sure, I'll fork over my share
to keep Elmo rocking for the young and tender

but for now I'm plumb slack-mouthed grateful
as Julia swirls the eggs in counterclockwise syncopation

all the while urging me
to enjoy the good life which

according to her
is as imminently accessible

as the gold just beyond that alabaster shell.

All I have to do is crack it open
drop those globes of gladness

into the waiting bowl
and whisk my way to bliss.

With disarming enthusiasm
Julia asserts that cooking isn't complicated at all

but simply a matter of reaching for what we want:
a perfectly roasted *côte du boeuf*

a luxuriant stretch of phyllo
a basket of succulent chanterelles!

Voilà: Earthly satisfaction.

I love Julia's conviction
her *sans souci* claim on nature's opulent gifts.

I love the way every expert rotation
coagulating that sun

is a nudge in the ribs to *Care less. Indulge more.*
I believe her unspoken assertion that

le paradis
is just one chopped chive garnish away.

So let us eat—yes!—with abandon
licking the frosting from the back of the spoon

nipping at the brandy
wallowing in the luscious gravy of life.

Pilates After 50

Working the belly
is like punching rising dough

back into the bowl. The resistance
will not be televised (thank God).

Now legs, with hamstrings tight as Royal Gorge cables.
My dancing dog

has been hit with buckshot.
Next up: planks.

From the shaking bridge of my body
I look down. My pendulous belly

sways in the breeze. Foot cramps.
Corpse pose for 30 seconds. (60. 100. 120.)

I dig deep, execute 30 decent pushups
on my knees. My reward is ab work:

Lower, upper. Shoulders to knees—"Work it!"
I'm a lumpy ninja school dropout.

Now shoulders and biceps. Time to burn this mother down!
(No really, it burns.)

In the shower
I can barely lift my arms to shampoo.

A glance at the clock gets my heart rate up again.
Late again. I reach for the towel—Wait...what's that?

My arms wave back at me, taut and sleek. My shoulders wink.
Well, hello there, beautiful.

Kitchen Confession

The poet is just as often known
for what's not said
the burgeoning thoughts left
nestled between words
startled revelations that rise up
from the tall grass of imagery
                    like flushed doves.

But so often my tongue flaps like the wings of a falcon on a jess
or a hen in a Chinese market
just this side of dinner, doom pressing in like a shopper
and only my clucking to keep disaster at bay.

Some days the best poems aren't words at all
but more sensory and tangible
like this spicy Bulgarian tomato soup I just made
lumpy with couscous dumplings
        touched with dill.

Take a bite.
Exhale poetry
through every pore.

Book Club

This is what we tell the husbands:
>*I need some time to expand my mind.*
>*I am joining a book club.*
And we do: All across America we meet
in living rooms vacated by solicitous mates.
In church basements and cozy rented cabins
we gather to pour over plots and characters
philosophies and intrigue.
Bolstered with questions and theories
we arrive with our sturdy canvas book bags.

And sister, we drink. From those dowdy library totes
we pull wine and tequila bottles in quantities
that would arch even Mary Poppins' brow.
With a cackle worthy of Lady MacBeth
we uncork, unstopper
loosen our Grecian belts
and drink.

Of course, our intellectual endeavors
are international in scope: Nebbiolo, Tempranillo
Shiraz and of course *Champagne.*
We expound on the virtues of
French Brie and Belgian chocolate. Queso and chips.
Reading glasses flung into a bowl like car keys at an orgy
we laugh like Brontë women released from lunatic attics
wild-haired sisters cut lose from the gloomy moors.

Other ladies—PTA darlings, carpool troopers—
hear of our devotion to Book Club and ask *What are you reading?*
Eyes hopeful for an invite
their smiles belie their Oprah aesthetics.
Oh, we're working our way through the classics
we say, and their expressions disintegrate like papyrus

in Caesar's Alexandria. And then for good measure:
Right now we're studying the Russians.
(And how! Stoli, Beluga, Limonnaya—our syllabus is martini
    rigorous.)

So what if *The Great Gatsby* is really The Great Excuse?
We like our irony dramatic, thank you.
And literature courses with no final
just endless
painstaking research.

Lupini for Breakfast

for Clinio

Invisible face, I miss you.
I eat lupini for breakfast
      snacking on their saltiness
      the legume-y heartiness of them.

You used to sit across from me
      at this very table.
We made attempts at knowing each other
      across this sticky vinyl tablecloth
      peppered with bread crumbs
drinking from jelly jars
red wine hauled up from the barrel in the cellar.

Since you've gone I am too terrified
      to love anything up close.
I need distance to feel the sting of it.
Perhaps I am practicing for the inevitable
      because in the end someone always
      disappears in an elaborate three-day puff of smoke.
      Holy or sane, there is no in-between.
Eventually one is left to eat lupini
      popping the hard, smooth bean out of its slick jacket
      crunching that salty yellow disk
      with a vaguely disgruntled gratification

      chewing those tears.

To an Unlabeled Bottle of Viognier

You boast an American vintage of a feisty harvest
packed with Colorado minerals
and busting with Rocky Mountain sunshine.
Young and bold in your assertions of florals and flint
you remind me of a duded-up cowboy
high on horse sweat and liquor and the perfume of
globe-breasted Gunnison gals with bright blonde hair
and come-hither hips poured into denim.
In that first sip a hint of toast recalls
whiskers that scratched my young neck
under a full-to-bursting moon, then your boisterous fruit
fills the mouth, its bawdy, bulging
grapiness cries out for grilled mahi mahi
slathered in dill mayonnaise, crowned with
rings of red onion on a crusty Kaiser roll.
You see? You want to flaunt your Americanness
but you court cultures of Polynesia
and the very Teutons who overlorded your ancestors
and you forget. who. I. am. I knew your great-great-
great-great-great-grandfather, made love to him
on the banks of the Rhône, fed him only Brie
and baguette, the occasional pear and
blackberries picked by the side of that dusty road
outside Condrieu. I wonder what he would think
of you, so yippee-ai-ay in your glass saddle.
To test you, I eat one fat twisted lariat of a
Cheeto, the biggest hammer I can find in my pantry today
and you—you insolent brat—
    slug
    me
    back.
Well done, my friend. Well done.
Your forebears would be proud.

can I get a witness?

Leap of Faith

Today a 40-year-old single mother
comes into the Writing Center for help on a paper.
Maybe every tenth word is spelled correctly.
She says shyly,
> *My grandmother locked me*
> *in her apartment every day until 3:00*
> *so I couldn't attend school.*
> *She said teachers could be cruel.*
Her words pool around us.
Sometimes all you can do is witness.

At age 23 she locked *herself* in a room
this time with a Holy Bible
for three days and three nights.
Wouldn't come out
until the lines and dots coalesced into stories.
> *That was God's first miracle for me.*
> *I told Him, if you exist, show me how to read.*

It takes time to decipher her grade-schooler scrawl
        the spelling that shouts her phonetic gifts.
A story
carefully shaped
sincerely told:
> Her daughter wants to run away
> with a boy
get married at the ripe age of 13.

The shapes of her letters
teeter earnestly across the page
puppies clamoring over each other
eager to be held in human hands.

I say, *You can do this.*
Here's how you build on the words you know:
> *Hope. Birth. Blessing. God.*

How My Prayer Changed

for Anthony, Austin, and Athena, ages 6, 4, and 2

When I read about the man
who drowned his own children
in a hotel bathroom

so their mother would have to live
without them

when I thought of the little faces
    she had cupped
    in her hands a thousand times

looking up at *him*
through the water

as one by one
he did the unthinkable

I prayed first that God
would welcome them
    through the churn and the
    last slow bubbles
as little ones come in from the snow

that feeling of immediate relief
    when powdered snow pants
        soggy mittens and wet boots

        are peeled off
        so toes and fingers can thaw

then just as quickly
I prayed they'd forget

soft pajamas
    the smooth satin edges of blankies
        the scent of her skin
            as she bent to kiss them
            good-night

any *thing* of this earth

I wanted them to know only
shapeless warmth, buoyant comfort
no longing or fear

small recompense

for those horrible last hours

those terrible big hands.

Guernica Unveiled

*On the second floor of the United Nations building in
Manhattan, just outside the Security Council entrance,
hangs a seminal piece of 20th-century artwork that offers
a graphic and chilling reminder of the horrors of war.*

*But as U.S. Secretary of State Colin Powell sat down last
week to deliver an historic speech about why America must
go to war with Iraq, Pablo Picasso's* Guernica *was
concealed by a large blue drape.*

> —*Published in the* Toronto Star
> *on Sunday, February 9, 2003*

In my dream the black hand of silence
closes around my throat.
At the other end of the arm
is my family
by blood and marriage
whom you have duped
with your cheerleader rhetoric
and slick presentations
of twisted data and perverted half-truths.
These are the crimes you will pay for:
for dividing a house
for annexing imagination
for exploiting a nation
of people longing to prolong
the illusion
that any ass that needs kicking
will answer to our lonely boot.

The billions of dollars I can forgive you.
Even the tailspin into economic ruin.
A lean diet, after all, brings clarity.
But the relentless deception
the alienation of reason

the traps loaded with American bodies
the hungering babies
the widowed mothers
the gaping maw of hell blooming on earth:
No.

I loosen the hand.
You can buy
all the air time you want.
You will not disassemble
my country of truth.

How to Negotiate with a Madman

1.

First, you must have something he wants. Oil fields, diamond mines, access to other countries' borders. Something that ultimately he will lunge for. He must lunge because every lunge happens over an abyss. You need the abyss.

2.

Practice your sneer. It must be cold and impenetrable, so he will respect you. Try to look as if you are wiping your feet on the backs of the oppressed. Madmen love that look.

3.

When you meet, casually flash some insignificant but prestigious object that is much cooler than his own fashionable object. You know, a more stylish watch, better cigars, a prettier woman. A little spark of jealousy will keep his attention without stirring his ire.

4.

Offer your madman refreshments. Be sure they are appropriate—many madmen are teetotalers, since they have to watch their backs. Others are easily distracted with a vial of white powder. Know who you are dealing with.

5.

If your madman has any personal ticks—a germ phobia or an aversion to pretzels—show respect by avoiding any reference to same. Always accommodate without drawing attention to the problem.

6.

Sprinkle your opening conversation with bloated compliments. Be Biblical in proportion. Say, "How glorious is your name all over the earth!" Reassure the madman that you understand intimately his private concerns. Say, "Be not vexed over evildoers." Make it sound like you're on the same team.

7.

Do not use reports, charts, or evidence when dealing with a madman. Details only bore him. In particular, do not mention such annoyances as the vulnerable, the displaced, the so-called civilian "casualties." Madmen do not concern themselves with people who place themselves in the wrong place at the wrong time.

8.

As your negotiations progress, make your compliments more mystical and slightly confusing. Say, "You have the wisdom of a million shrunken heads." Say, "The javelina is myopic, but the rooster speaks truth at dawn."

9.

If you approach an impasse, divert. Offer obscure references as nuggets of pure wisdom. Say, "The whip for the horse, the bridle for the ass, and the rod for the backs of fools." Then raise your eyebrows and say, "I think you know what I mean." If tensions arise, say "The witchery of paltry things obscures what is right."

10.

Every step of your negotiations with the madman must be toward the desired precipice. Lure him carefully but steadily. Keep him slightly off-balance. Zig when he zags. Freeze when he charges. If his focus wavers, push hard. Harder.

11.

Abuse language. Say "joy" when you mean fear, as in, "Your people embrace you with joy." Say "security" when you mean "oppression," as in, "We must ensure the people's security." Say "democracy" as if it is an experiment, the results of which you will later author yourself.

12.

If he makes some remark of disturbing content, say (grimly), "Your mother must be ashamed of you!" Then laugh wildly, knowingly.

13.

Make smaller and smaller concessions. To do this you must learn the proper math of negotiations. The lives of a hundred children are nothing to a dictator. The blood of a thousand soldiers is less precious than two extra minutes tacked onto a televised speech to hand a mother a solemnly folded flag. Keep your eyes on the prize, man.

14.

Do not become the madman. Make a stone wall around your heart. Do not strangle the neighbor's daughter with your bare hands just to see what it feels like. At least not where anyone can see you. Learn to wash your hands very carefully. Remember, the world is watching.

Disclosure

What the fuck do you believe in? Life demanded
as it slammed my skull into the sidewalk.

The back of my head
where the vision starts

occipital revelations
deep-rooted icons

not smoke but the mirrors.
Tangible symbols

and verifiable realities
all firing off the same motherboard.

The cement was cold
my shock complete.

Somewhere my feet were apologizing
for not paying attention.

I saw not stars but birds
zooming sparrows diving in random swoops.

My neck (captain's wheel of perception)
was already organizing protests.

What the fuck
did I believe in?

Only the cold arms of December
the wail of a distant siren

the warm and spreading pool
that ferried me over

to the other side
of hospital light.

Park-n-Ride

Safe behind "I told you so"
you toil away at your exile
insistent on your perfect futility
your perfect excuse.
I don't want to go through this again:
another saboteur off through the bus terminal.
You think you're traveling light
but there's your carrion luggage
your dead-weight habit.
Where's your muscle, damn it?
Because of you I ride buses all night
drive my car into snow banks again and again
take planes to frozen countries
show up without currency
speaking all the wrong languages.
Don't you get it? I pack suitcases
after you, fold socks over passports
forget my destination, my toothbrush—
I get on the wrong line
with only one shoe
see my past go by in the window
dressed in French finery
dining on Käsetorte and spumante
at little white tables
where the sea wears the shore down
to a thin, crisp wafer.

Meanwhile, back in your landlocked city
securely cynical in a dead man's coat
you play hide-and-seek with your
befuddled past, your foggy future.
You leap from one to the other
so your feet never touch the present.
Don't love me, don't love me, you chant.

You want to tangle yourself in the blankets
wrestle romantically with your failures
your mock triumphs, your hidden costs.
Infatuated with irresolution
you've got a bubble over your head.
If someone kissed it, it would pop
rain fairy-tale juice all over you
and there you'd be
a normal human being
with a man's job to do
the spell broken and nothing but
work work work
conform to the new and undesirably familiar.
Oh God, it could mean
an investment, a risk, you might
end up on TV, or worse: content.
You might have to wait for love
like some of us wait for the bus.

Full Moon with Heartache

for SFC Aaron Grider, killed in Afghanistan
on his 30th birthday, September 18, 2010

Full Moon raps on my window. "Are you up?"
I am now, wading out of my dreams of flooding.
How suddenly the waters rose while we were hiking
sending everyone scrambling for the banks.
In the brochures the waters were blue and green, serene
but by foot they are muddy, dark, rushing.
Full Moon tries again.
"Everyone dreams their own Katrina now.
But I've got bears and breezes out here."

I get up, look outside. No bears.
Trees nod in the breeze that slips through the window frame.
I pull my robe tighter, think of his bride
now surrounded by family
and of her friends now half a world away
on a trip she was supposed to join them on
—a distraction to while away his deployment.
They got the news
just hours before departure. Too late to cancel
too awful to go forward. What do you do?

I make the rounds, tuck in my sleeping babies.
Kiss foreheads, stare for a long time, grateful.
I check on the dog sacked out in her crate.
She breathes slowly, deeply
like the wound in our hearts.

Full Moon waits for me back in our room.
Husband sleeps, as always, with abandon.
Full Moon strokes his face with her silver hands.
She seems to need to talk. She sees a lot.

"I know you have more stories," I say.
But Full Moon stays quiet.
Hers is an ancient ache.
Finally, "The Alps," she offers.
"They were lovely tonight
beside the Wolfgangsee."

There is nothing I can say.
But words are not the point.

We sit and stare at the landscape together
two women
praying for peace
all the way to dawn.

Deliver the Medicine

You might never race
across the Arctic tundra
in January
bearing the antidote
for a lethal disease
your lungs burning with ice fog
as a storm rolls in from Norton Sound.

Pray you never
run to your death
through gale-force winds
that plunge the chill factor
to 85 below.

But if you ever find your grip
frozen in an exigent task
may you feel the heat
of the challenge
to make it in time.

Rest warm when you can
but with one ear cocked
for the truth is
we are all called
to deliver the medicine
to the stranger
the desperate
regardless of who is there
to witness
or not.

We are called
when the risk is great
the journey long
conditions horrid.

Mush mush, you faithful!
Deliver the medicine.
Deliver the day.

all the way to just about there

Vigil

You, who I carried
across the waters
to the island of us

you, who I cradled
first in my pelvis
then in my arms

you, who I held
tiny and diapered
across my chest
skin to skin
to keep you warm

lie here now
bathed in the pale green glow
of monitors and pumps

while the hallway light
spills under the door
to pool here
around IV pole casters

and your too-big
tiger-shaped slippers
tucked under the bed.

I watch your pulse
race across the screen
an endless mountain range
chasing its own shadow.

I watch numbers fall
then rise as you stir
when I place my hand
on your slender arm
with the tubes
spilling out of its crease.

Your chest barely moves
with each slow breath
as the Benadryl pulls you down
down below the turbulent wake

of colliding medicines
that minutes earlier
tossed you about
on the swells of hallucination.

"The walls are melting!" you cried
and swiped at the tube
snaking into your nose

thrashed against my arms
and hands that reached
to calm and secure
but frightened you instead.

So this is where we are, I think
and rub my eyes, my face.

I lower the bedrail
and climb onto your raft
stretch out along
your small curled shape.

We'll wait here together
in the dark
floating, waiting for that
message in a bottle
a map
to home.

Atomic Hearts

When the Titanic
    —steaming through the starlit night
    and bristling air—
charged headlong towards it

the iceberg sat there
mute, crippled
up to its neck
in black water.

Don't you think
if it had arms to wave
it would have tried
to ward off that disastrous ending
to invention's most audacious tale?

And the Hindenburg.
Silent, floating mourner—
how it must have anguished
over its passengers
even as the flames licked its skin
from the bowed metal ribs.

What if things "insensate"
actually do have feelings?
What if we could hear
tiny screams of terror
between the tightly bonded molecules
of iron and steel?

How could their atomic hearts
not be moved
by the cries of all those lost souls?

Nice Work If You Can Get It

"I'm celebrated for celebrating the uncelebrated."
—Studs Terkel

in that sense he was a poet, wasn't he?
for what do we do but uplift   the overlooked
hold it to the light

like the beggar   who
sticks his legs out   across the sidewalk
disrupting others' reverie   with uncomfortable truth

the child   talking loudly   shoves the bug
in the grown-up's face   insisting
look

the lone protester   outside
the high glass windows of the Drake
throws a rock   into the cocktail party

we just can't agree with the world   on priorities
prize prophets   over profits—
just look at our work   how it plods along
the topography of the heart
taking notes   endless notes

lazy with wonder   heavy with metaphor
we don't get up when   the bell rings
leave the windows open   all through the storm

you can't rely on us
when the laundry needs tending
the grass is overgrown
and now the phone keeps ringing...

hopelessly preoccupied
we stare at the fine line of light
that caresses the piano on a late September noon

study the fuzz on a crocus stem

memorize with eyes closed
the squirm and eager   salty breath of a warm puppy

we read the world in Braille
with our hands   our mouths

we feel the thrum and undercurrent
of the unspoken
our ears pressed to the silence
listening to the thundering approach
of the invisible

After the Fire

Eager to witness meteors
in a bright spill of stars

unspoiled by city lights
we traveled across

two wildfire footprints
to Buffalo Creek.

In the afternoon sun we
pitched our tents on the edge

of the burn area, then wandered in
to survey the damage.

More than a decade
into this new century

the scar from the last one was fresh.

We walked silently
through the cathedral of destruction

charred tree trunks still standing
their desiccated innards exposed

like books standing on end
the pages fanning out

in vertical chunks
we broke off without effort.

Stories printed in wood pulp
baked to meringue.

The still-shot landscape

was now spotted with new growth
doggedly marching through:

fireweed and columbines
bees and seedlings.

Death reluctantly yielding to life
at the speed of evolution.

That night we searched
for the cold fire of stars

for enflamed dust specks streaking the black
in their violent descent through atmosphere.

The smoke from our fire ascended to a clouded sky.

The Alchemy of Memory

Love, I long to dip you
in the bath of remove
dissolve all your faults in the
(oh) well of detachment.

Like a table with one short leg
you have wobbled through this day
tipping over the salt shaker of my tolerance
spilling all my consolation
that you are indeed only human.

Quit looking at me like that.
Quit leaving the door open
for blame to rush in.

Just go away for a while
so my sweet forgetful heart
can call you back
unchanged
but cherished
like gold.

The Abenaki word for "clock" is *babizookwazik*

I'll never forget the day you swaggered into my life
with your Russian accent and Roy Orbison glasses.
Your sideburns were sculpted
into a perfect bas-relief of an empanada.
The moment you first locked your lips on mine
and breathed your fire into my nascent lungs

I felt the stars blink on in my head
felt the earth rush past under my feet.
So this is what it's like, I thought
to be a balloon animal twisted into being
by the hands of a clown.

Those early days were miraculous.
Daisies blossomed in your footsteps.
Huge aquamarines dripped from your fingers.
"Go like this!" you whispered, urgent
as you waved your arms in the air like a maestro.
By the window, in the fruit bowl, the grapes burst their skins.

By the time we moved into the Quonset hut
all the china buffalo were broken
the coffee table recklessly tattooed with the water rings
of a thousand late-night parties.
"The cord's frayed," you accused
standing beneath the neon on the wall.

Burma Shave, it blinked. *Burma Shave.*

When You're Not Here

for Joe

My heart doesn't know what to do.
It drinks too much coffee
      twiddles its thumbs
sits by the phone.

It jumps every time the dog barks.

Outside, even the plants are confounded.
The Russian sage stares into the glare of noon

like a woman who has just walked into a room
and can't remember why.

The brooding geraniums nod dumbly on the breeze.
The pansies try their best to rustle, look important
      but who do they think they're fooling?
Even the rain won't fall when you're not here.

The children squabble and play with their food.
Hummingbirds dive at each other
in irritable swoops.

The crows complain loudly
the fox slinks away in disgust

and everything—even the impervious pines—

waits for your return.

Unfinished Business

"Ask me whether what I have done is my life."
—*William Stafford*

An enormous catalog of to-do's
you cannot read.
    Cross-outs and edits
scribbles in the margins—extraneous thoughts
    so ripe with potential brilliance
they run up the sides of the paper
    in loopy script.
Crammed between the lines
    a scrawl so full of *passion* and conviction(!)
it slants right off the page.

    Asterisks and footnotes
taped-in pages and folded-down corners.
    Very few doodles
but each an epiphany, if I remember correctly.

Cover tattered—raggedy
    and getting worse.
Pages anointed with melted butter.
    Doesn't matter—
you can't handle this sprawling tome
    anyway.
Even I can hardly manage
    its sloppy glory
    its unfathomable grace.

The Interpreter of Birds

for Murray Moulding

I go into the forest to listen.
A folding chair, a beer, two ears.

First, the raucous flies
industriously nosy.

What have I brought them?
Only a little sweat ruined with sunscreen.

Still they return often
to see if my story has changed.

A fat bumblebee, orange as beetle kill
drifts by heavy and low, a lazy zeppelin

buzzing toward some sweeter pasture.
The flies continue their gossip

as if I were some tangy-sweet small-town distraction
as if they lived somewhere boring.

In the distance, songbirds have strung
a highway of language between the trees.

They race along it back and forth
returning each other's calls as if to say

I forgot to mention—
only to repeat themselves.

I listen hard to decipher their patois
but only the skilled ear can hear the news in a tongue

with neither vowels nor consonants
formed without the aid of lips.

I struggle as they twitter and loop
draping their thoughts from tree to tree.

They are upset or joyful
about events disturbing or miraculous:

perhaps the dying forest
the falling price of twigs

the need for a cure for all these flies.
Or maybe the way this summer day

unrolls like a wave
renewing itself by the moment.

I wish for my friend with the gift
to translate what disturbs their delicate hearts—

rumors or dire warnings
idle chatter or just a poem like this one

interrupted by flies
when there is so much to talk about:

the cloudless sky, the molting pines, the ageless valley
and everything in between.

Tiny Islands

When my life resembles a scowling dwarf
peering around a big dark door

when circumstance puts up a speed bump
or my tires slip in the mud *again*

I dream of moving to an island
a tropical la-la land
like Maui or...Maui.

Or maybe the Big Island.
Someplace far but not too foreign
and anchored with an adequate earthy bulk
because I admit: I need the security of gravity.

When I look on the *National Geographic Map of the World*
at some of those smaller dots, my head spins.
I could live on a smudge but never a pinpoint.
Okay, I know that there are actually people on
say, St. Croix or St. Thomas
        and they have cars
        and even telephones.
But those *teeny* dots?
Like those freckles they call Micronesia.
Just the name makes me nervous.
And look at the Cook Islands
        so far adrift in their million square miles
        of nothing but ocean
they may as well be planets.
Their tiny swells can barely uphold
the skinny letters straddling their slight girth:
        Aitutaki, Mitiaro, Manihiki.
You could drop off into open water
trying to walk across all those i's and t's.

So while I want to escape
all the snowstorms and hailstones
life can sling my way
if I were completely untethered
from my petty daily struggles
I would panic.
Like the astronauts working in space   I could be lost.
Even aboard the mothership
weeks of weightless floating
make their muscles atrophy.
                        Like stretched taffy
their spines elongate. Their bones thin.
Weak as patients
they have to reacclimate slowly
or perish.
And those are the lucky ones.
Some really do spin off into oblivion:
      the Challenger crew careening into the afterlife
      the Columbia crew disintegrating over Texas
      and Louisiana, just this close to finishing the job.
They thought they were off to conduct
hundreds of new experiments
when in fact
      they *were* the experiment
the same experiment we all have to try:
How far can you go
and still come back alive?

all the way to just about there

Four in the morning
and things missing from my bloodstream
cause a clanging through my veins

a rowdy protest of longing.
Outside it's no better:

      the endless rise and swell
      of cars along the highway below

      slick serpents hissing their discontent
      slithering along in angry pursuit
      of the missing.

Higher up the drone of airplanes
drilling through the night.
They appear to be flying

but they're just falling along the curve of the Earth
      homesick for her primal pull
      displacing air for the absent.

      Once there was an astronaut
who fell in love with longing
the endless quest for perfection.
She put miles of achievement behind her
      feeding an emptiness that fueled her
      through the darkness
and crashed headlong into madness.

      Even in space
      the thing that's missing
      weighs heavy on the heart.

So satellites, like distant cries
race along under the skin of night
in search of connection

decipherable contact
with the invisible

    and anyone who's ever lost anything
    is awake with me tonight
    dragging our tin cups
    across the bars of our loss

while other searchers
    barrel through the dark
    hoping to spill out into the light

    and weightlessness

      at last.

Acknowledgments

The author would like to thank the editors of the print and online publications in which the following poems first appeared.

Elevated Living: "May in Evergreen"
Glass: A Journal of Poetry: "Nice Work If You Can Get It,"
    "all the way to just about there"
Kinesis: "Park-n-Ride"
Mad Blood: "To an Unlabeled Bottle of Viognier"
Marathon Literary Review: "Where I Come From"
Mothers Always Write: "For Sarah, Driving to the PSAT,"
    "I Tell Her Every Day She's Beautiful"
Poets Against War: "*Guernica* Unveiled"
Reunion: The Dallas Review: "Leap of Faith"
Sniper Logic: "Lupini for Breakfast"
Steam Ticket: "Blood on the Motel Sidewalk," "In April"
Word Riot: "The Abenaki word for 'clock' is *babizookwazik*"
Word Soup: "Call Now and Receive This Classic 4-DVD Set!"

The author is incredibly grateful for the love and support of Rita Brady Kiefer, Joseph Hutchison, Jim Keller, and Murray Moulding; and for the support of my colleagues at Red Rocks Community College. I am privileged to be in community with such amazing humans.

About FutureCycle Press

FutureCycle Press is dedicated to publishing lasting poetry books, chapbooks, and anthologies in English in both print-on-demand and Kindle ebook formats. Founded in 2007 by long-time independent editor/publishers and partners Diane Kistner and Robert S. King, the press incorporated as a nonprofit in 2012. A number of our editors are distinguished poets and writers in their own right, and we have been actively involved in the small press movement going back to the early seventies.

The FutureCycle Poetry Book Prize and honorarium is awarded annually for the best full-length volume of poetry we publish in a calendar year. Introduced in 2013, our Good Works projects are anthologies devoted to issues of universal significance, with all proceeds donated to a related worthy cause. Our Selected Poems series highlights contemporary poets with a substantial body of work to their credit; with this series we strive to resurrect work that has had limited distribution and is now out of print.

We are dedicated to giving all of the authors we publish the care their work deserves, making our catalog of titles the most diverse and distinguished it can be, and paying forward any earnings to fund more great books.

We've learned a few things about independent publishing over the years. We've also evolved a unique, resilient publishing model that allows us to focus mainly on vetting and preserving for posterity poetry collections of exceptional quality without becoming overwhelmed with bookkeeping and mailing, fundraising activities, or taxing editorial and production "bubbles." To find out more about what we are doing, come see us at www.futurecycle.org.

The FutureCycle Poetry Book Prize

All full-length volumes of poetry published by FutureCycle Press in a given calendar year are considered for the annual FutureCycle Poetry Book Prize. This allows us to consider each submission on its own merits, outside of the context of a contest. Too, the judges see the finished book, which will have benefitted from the beautiful book design and strong editorial gloss we are famous for.

The book ranked the best in judging is announced as the prize-winner in the subsequent year. There is no fixed monetary award; instead, the winning poet receives an honorarium of 20% of the total net royalties from all poetry books and chapbooks the press sold online in the year the winning book was published. The winner is also accorded the honor of being on the panel of judges for the next year's competition; all judges receive copies of all contending books to keep for their personal library.